QUOTES

OF

ONE

DIRECTION

Funny, inspirational & motivational quotations of One Direction

Terms Of Use Agreement

Every effort had been made to fulfill requirements with regard to reproducing copyrighted material. The author and the publisher will be glad to certify any omissions at the earliest opportunity.

Disclaimer

The author and the publisher have used their best efforts in preparing this book. The author and the publisher make no representation or warranties with respect to the accuracy, fitness, applicability, or completeness of the contents of this work and specifically disclaim all warranties, including without limitation warranties of fitness for a particular purpose. This work is sold with the understanding that author and the publisher is not engaged in rendering legal, or any other professional services.

My sister used to call me Cheesy-Head because I loved these cheesy crisps
— Liam Payne

From day one, we said that we don't want to try and be anything that we're not, and none of us are dancers.
— Niall Horan

When I first got with the boys Niall would fart all the time and I wasn't used to that. But you just get used to it, you learn how to be a lad.
— Zayn Malik

We're not perfect, we're not clean cut. We're trying to be ourselves
— Louis Tomlinson

They have been so successful on two separate occasions, they're basically a British institution now. It would be amazing even if we could just have a tiny bit of the success that they have achieved.
— Louis Tomlinson, talking about Take That

I was never really a fan of boy bands before One Direction
— Louis Tomlinson

I think my musical idols are Elvis and Michael Jackson.
— Zayn Malik

Just being about to take part and how much your confidence grows each week being up there performing in front of the judges.
— Louis Tomlinson

They kind of told us that we were too good to let go, so they'd just put us in a group.
— Niall Horan

I'm talking about harry so much these days, but my love to — Liam Payne will never change aha ;)
— Zayn Malik

If you're feeling a bit down, come and talk to Daddy Liam
— Louis Tomlinson

If i'm louder would you see me?
— Niall Horan

Harry loves to steal food off people's plates, but he is too scared to do it to Niall.
— Louis Tomlinson

Once I was taking shower and heard a noise, so I opened the curtains and there was Niall sitting on the toilet. He just said Hi.
— Zayn Malik

If I was in a horror film I'd die first, because I would have no idea what's going on.
— Niall Horan

My trademark saying is probably VAS HAPPENIN?!
— Zayn Malik

When Zayn is tired, he won't care who you are, he will sleep on your shoulder.
— Liam Payne

Once we were eight hours without eating, so Louis took out a cereal bar, and instead of eating it, he gave it to me.
— Niall Horan

Wow, Take Me Home is number 1 in Sweden, Holland, Germany, Australia, New Zealand, Belgium, Norway and Switzerland! thats so awesome!!! :)
— Louis Tomlinson

Little Things isn't about anyone in particular, it's about girls, you all are beautiful and you need to hear it more often.
— Zayn Malik

You're going to see lot more of what we're like when we interact with each other behind the scenes and it's a nice insight.
— Harry Style

There is only so much you can offer on a social media, Twitter and a five-minute interview. So we wanted to really give behind-the-scenes access to all areas, documentary and it's like for us, what it's like for our

families, and what these guys have done really in three years.
— Niall Horan

A nice look at our families, as well. The way that they deal with us being away from home.
— Liam Payne

Wrote my first song ever today alone, maybe i'll sing it someday when i go solo hahaha who knows :) x
— Zayn Malik

We get quite a lot of random things thrown on stage—I mean, they throw iPhones.
— Zayn Malik

It's so amazing to hear a crowd of people singing one of your songs. It's the best feeling.
— Liam Payne

I do miss home. People don't appreciate where they come from until they go back. I love going home now.
— Niall Horan

Someone sent me a toilet seat for my birthday.
— Harry Styles

Fans aren't just fans... they're part of my family
— Zayn Malik

Our girls are pretty, I would marry them all.
— Harry Styles

Feel free to insult me, but you don't have the right to insult our fans.
— Louis Tomlinson

Even when I'm sleeping, I'm dreaming about meeting fans.
— Liam Payne

I like a good smile, good sense of humor, someone who I can actually have a chat with and not be awkward around. Nice eyes ... Kate Beckinsale
— Niall Horan

Don't ever let a guy make you feel ugly because no matter what you are beautiful with or without him-—Zayn Malik
— Zayn Malik

I was really short and she was really tall, so I had to put a brick against the wall and stand on it to reach her face.
— Zayn Malik, about the first kiss

I'd rather be called a boy and play with paper airplanes than be called a man and play with a girl's heart.
— Niall Horan

I like chilled out, relaxed girls who don't take life too seriously.
— Zayn Malik

I like girls who eat carrots
— Louis Tomlinson

Sometimes, the girls hug all the boys except me, and I just smile, but it hurts.
— Niall Horan

I want a girl who doesn't know she's beautiful, so I have an excuse to let her know all the time.
— Zayn Malik

I had my first kiss when I was 11, but I think I've blocked it out of my mind because it was so bad. I'm not even sure it counts as a kiss.
— Niall Horan

If a man whistles at you, don't turn around, ignore him. You're lady, not a dog.
— Niall Horan

My accent always work with girls. They like it. I have no idea why.
— Niall Horan

I want a girl who doesn't know she's beautiful, so I have an excuse to let her know all the time.
— Zayn Malik

My mum doesn't have a twitter account, she dont even know how to use a computer hahahaha :) x
— Zayn Malik

Now that I have my Rose, I really do have everything I could ever want, I have family, romance, friends, fans, and im just surrounded by love.
— Zayn Malik

I actually haven't been on many dates, but I like just chilling around at home and watching a movie with a girl.
— Niall Horan

I won't date a model, because models are perfect and perfect is boring.
— Niall Horan

I flirt but i also sleep in my own bed.xx
— Harry Styles

I'm the kind of boy that can fall in love with any girl because I love with the heart, not the eyes.
— Niall Horan

Oh it's the bingo playing wizard.I love you guys so much, but not as much as my bird and my bingo!
— Louis Tomlinson

I wish I had a girl to cuddle up to at night rather than my pillow
— Harry Styles

If my girlfriend needs anything. I'm always here for her.
— Zayn Malik

I don't think you can define love.
— Harry Styles

The biggest downside for us is being away from home, missing our families, them missing us, we know it comes with the job and then when we are with our families I miss these gusy, so you kind of win.
— Liam Payne

Once you learn to truly appreciate what you do have then you can begin to deserve what you want. x
— Zayn Malik

There comes a day when you realise turning the page is the best feeling in the world, because you realise there's so much more to the book than the page you were stuck on.
— Zayn Malik

Give it up for Harry Pottery
— Niall Horan

You can't go to sleep without a cup of tea and maybe that's the reason that you talk in your sleep...
— Louis Tomlinson

Live life to the fullest because everything else is uncertain
— Louis Tomlinson

If you want to do something, Go for it you've got nothing to lose
— Louis Tomlinson

We have a choice..To Live or To Exist
— Harry Styles

I give great hugs!
— Niall Horan

I'll always defend the people I love.
— Niall Horan

My biggest turn off is being a basic bitch. Damn, I hate basic bitches.
— Zayn Malik

I have had a haircut that I've regretted.
Liam

Who doesn't need an eraser? Everyone makes mistakes.
— Louis Tomlinson

I'd like to hug and kiss all our fans.
— Zayn Malik

Just because you don't have a prince, doesn't mean you're not a princess
— Zayn Malik

The strongest people aren't always the people who win, but the people who don't give up when they lose
— Liam Payne

Every day should be a new day.
— Harry Styles

Life, is hard, but if it weren't, where would the challenge be?
— Zayn Malik

Funny how everyone hates Muslims because of a few attacks. We need to open our eyes to who the real terrorists are.
— Zayn Malik

I don't think you can really define love
— Harry Styles

If it were legal, I'd marry food
— Niall Horan

Stop worrying about someone that isn't worried about you. Never leave your key of happiness in someone else's pockets x
— Zayn Malik

Live for who you are and what you love.
— Zayn Malik

Harry Styles, Hahaha i don't really consider myself as a celebrity, i still wear my old dirty converses! you forgot to mention your old dirty socks too! ;)
— Zayn Malik

I'm lucky my last name isn't balls.
— Harry Styles

Once again massive thankyou to you all, you are not just fans you are family... our family, 3 EMAs babe yeah man :)
— Liam Payne

Hello! I'm your host Louis The Tommo Tomlinson, I'm sat in a trolley because it makes no sense!
— Louis Tomlinson

Please excuse me while I say: We fucking love you guys!
— Louis Tomlinson

mission : going to annoy zayn till he wake up like the old days hahah i dont know but i just wanna do it
— Liam Payne

Watched harry potter yesterday and decided i want to be him ahaa
— Liam Payne

They don't know about us is about someone used to mean something to me, hopefully you like it!
— Liam Payne

I've always preferred having girlfriends to just seeing people.
— Liam Payne

I didn't really enjoy her fainting in front of me, it wasn't something that I enjoyed. However, it was pretty cool to know that I could make a girl faint. I'm not gonna lie.
— Zayn Malik

I once woke up at a random guys house and I didn't actually know who he was.
— Louis Tomlinson

I'll always defend the people I love, even though I'm as terrifying as a… as a… baby penguin?
— Niall Horan

Justin Bieber first followed Zayn and we ran to tell Niall who was in the shower. He came out running wet and started crying.
— Liam Payne

I was about to hug a fan, but she said she wanted to hug Louis. She was about to hug Louis, but Louis said he wanted to hug me.
— Niall Horan

A real girl isn't perfect, and a perfect girl isn't real.
— Harry Styles

Niall once argued with an airport security guard for 30 min so he could bring food on the plane.
— Zayn Malik

The creepiest thing about being famous is like, everyone's watching your every move. Especially when I'm eating.
— Niall Horan

I drew a cat recently and Louis asked me why I was drawing a giraffe.
— Harry Styles

Miss her smile, her giggle, miss being the one she couldn't wait to get home to talk to.
— Liam Payne

if i was really really gay, i'd marry ed.
— Harry Styles

Signing my first autograph was quite awkward because I didn't have one
— Harry Styles

Louis ate Niall's last chips when Niall went to the toilet, and Niall didn't talk to Louis for an hour...
— Zayn Malik

My favourite one in the group was Zayn, until he stole my meal. Now Harry is my favourite.
— Niall Horan

A short skirt and lots of make-up won't impress me.
— Harry Styles

Don't watch Gangnam Style video with Lux. She tries
and falls on her ass. Haha
Lou Teasdale

I want people to stay away from my ex
— Liam Payne

When you have many reasons to keep going,problems
will never destroy you. That's something I've learned
trough these years
— Harry Styles

Just invited myself to a dinner tonight. In in relationship
with myself.
— Harry Styles

We're not perfect, we're not clean cut. We're just trying
to be ourselves.
— Louis Tomlinson

It takes a second to call a girl fat and she'll take a
lifetime trying to stave herself. Think before you act.
— Harry Styles

I'd rather stay home and watch movies with a girl than
go out to a fancy restaurant.
— Niall Horan

I think ruth's dog and i are best friends now :)
— Liam Payne

Once I tried to eat without a spoon for a day and it was really hard. Liam is the man!
— Zayn Malik

A smile could last for a second but the memory of it could last for a last for a lifetime
— Liam Payne

It doesn't matter what other people think about you. The only thing that matters is that you are happy with who you are.
— Zayn Malik

We're just like normally silly teenagers, except that I'm not a teenager anymore which makes me really depressed.
— Louis Tomlinson

The sun is shining, it's a beautiful day, nothing like spending the day with your friends, and talking all night to someone you love.
— Zayn Malik

Our dolls were on the shelf and Justin Bieber's doll was next to us and his doll was taller than mine.
— Liam Payne

If Niall gives you his last chip you must be really special.
— Zayn Malik

Zayn sometimes pisses me off, how can he be so stunning without even trying!
— Niall Horan

We can be a bit immature at times, but I'm known as the mature one.
— Liam Payne

Being single doesn't mean that you're weak, it means that you're strong enough to wait for what you deserve.
— Niall Horan

Hello girls that are beautiful, but don't know it. Heads up, you're beautiful.
— Niall Horan

Liam once forgot the lyrics during the performance so he tapped on the microphone and pretended it wasn't working.
— Niall Horan

Tall girls are hot, little girls are cuties.
— Harry Styles

For my birthday I got a bike. It was difficult to ride, but I'm — Harry Styles.
— Harry Styles

Harry is the youngest, but everyone always think it's me.
— Niall Horan

You can usually hear me before you see me.
— Niall Horan

When Justin Bieber was following me, Niall sang That Should Be Me and when Justin Bieber followed him, Niall sang Never Say Never.
— Zayn Malik

It doesn't matter what other people think about you. The only thing that matters is that you are happy with who you are.
— Zayn Malik

Open up your eyes, then you'll realise, here I stand with my, everlasting love.
— Liam Payne

The person who will give you unexplained happiness will also give you unexplained sadness.
— Zayn Malik

Never live life in fear of death.
— Zayn Malik

I don't know if we'll ever get used to the attention from the fans
— Louis Tomlinson

I think the key is to not look like you tried too hard, but at the same time, try a little bit.
— Harry Styles

Before you judge people, judge yourself.
— Zayn Malik

I don't really think I've got anything specific other than the fact that i never wear socks
— Louis Tomlinson

My style is quite plain, I used to wear T-shirts and skinny jeans and stuff...
— Liam Payne

(I've smoked) since I was about 15.
— Zayn Malik

It's mad to think I didn't know them two years ago and now they're my best mates.
— Liam Payne

Big Bang Theory is hilarious aha!
— Zayn Malik

I'm not dating Leona Lewis don't trust those random source accounts on twitter :)
— Liam Payne

Danielle is great. I really hope we can still be friends
— Liam Payne

Dreams are like stars. You may never touch them, but if you follow them, they will lead you to your destiny.
— Liam Payne

I don't need the perfect one. I just need somebody who will make me feel like I'm the only one.
— Zayn Malik

Well, personally, I wouldn't like to be a food, because I wouldn't want to be eaten
— Niall Horan

Life's too short to be anything but happy. So take what you have and make the best of it.
— Zayn Malik

Frankly, I don't care what others say.
— Niall Horan

Got nothing to say, say nothing at all.
— Liam Payne

This doesn't happen to people from Mullingar.
— Niall Horan

If a guy is taking his girl for granted, he really deserves a slap, with a baseball bat.
— Louis Tomlinson

Truth is, I don't mind getting a black eye or broken arm for a girl as long as she's there to kiss it after.
— Harry Styles

I do miss home. People don't appreciate where they come from until they go back. I love going home now.
— Niall Horan

I once cried in a restaurant because the waitress told me I could not eat my soup with a fork. I had to use a spoon.
— Liam Payne

The challenges aren't there to stop you...they're there to help you grow
— Zayn Malik

Girls are the same all over the world, aren't they? They're all beautiful.
— Liam Payne

Live fast, have fun and be a bit mischievous
— Louis Tomlinson

She ripped out my heart, and threw it away. Given up on love, I just wanted to say. I love you, its true, there was noone but you.
— Zayn Malik

It's cool to know that I can make girls faint
— Zayn Malik

Never loved anyone in my life as much as that one person. didnt ever think a love so strong was possible
— Liam Payne

I came home one day and my turtle was missing a foot.
— Liam Payne

It's odd that girls ask if they can hug me. Don't ask, do it. I'm just a regular guy.
— Niall Horan

Dreams always come true, if you only believe.
— Zayn Malik

Faith can really help get you through the hard times.
— Zayn Malik

Niall is always hungry because he has an angel eating inside him. That's why he sings like one.
— Liam Payne

When you open Niall's wallet, the first thing you see is a picture of Justin Bieber and a picture of us
— Liam Payne

I've always wanted to be one of those people who didn't really care much about what people thought about them, but I just don't think I am
— Harry Styles

Applied for xfactor,hope it all wrks out
— Niall Horan

You say you want it, You love me then thought it.
You're breaking my heart... And you're taking me down.
— Niall Horan

Life is a gift, love it, live it.
— Zayn Malik

It hurts seeing a girl cry. I want to comfort them for as long as I can, or I'll end up crying too.
— Zayn Malik

Don't depend on someone promising you the world. Fulfill your own wishes, make your own dreams come true
— Zayn Malik

The hardest challenge is to be yourself in a world where everyone is trying to make you be somebody else
— Zayn Malik

My worst habit is getting naked all the time.
— Harry Styles

Until I meet my perfect girl, I have Louis.
— Harry Styles

Don't live in the past. You might miss the great things happening in your present.
— Zayn Malik

Good decisions come from experience, and experience comes from bad decisions.
— Zayn Malik

Liam, Harry, Niall and Louis are my brothers from another mother.
— Zayn Malik

You make life out of what you have, not what you're missing.
— Zayn Malik

The most valuable lessons in life cannot be taught, they must be experienced.
— Liam Payne

You always think there's someone missing in the band, because you never count yourself.
— Louis Tomlinson

There are 12 months a year...30 days a month...7 days a week...24 hours a day...60 minutes an hour...but only one like you in a lifetime.
— Liam Payne

You know when the sun forgets to shine I'll be there to hold you through the night And we'll be running so fast we can fly tonight And even when we're miles and miles apart You're still holding all of my heart I promise it will never be dark I know..we're inseparable
— Louis Tomlinson

Learn to appreciate what you have before time forces you to appreciate what you had
— Zayn Malik

Louis knows, I'm Bruce Lee
— Zayn Malik

I really shouldn't be saying this, but once me and Liam were fooling around and we ended up kissing
— Zayn Malik

Don't download LWWY, buy it for us
— Harry Styles

Cats Are Evil. They Just Sit There And Look At You, You Know Theyre Plotting World Domination, Just Waiting For The Moment To Pounce.
— Liam Payne

Life, is hard, but if it weren't, where would the challenge be?
— Zayn Malik

My faith means everything to me, god is sending me on this journey, this discovery, of who I am, and I trust his judgement. x
— Zayn Malik

When I was small I had a desk, it was weird because I wrote in it, 'When I grow up, I wanna be a singer'. I, like, inscribed it in, and it's still on the desk.
— Niall Horan

When I was little I knew that I wanted to entertain people. I was a proper show off.
— Harry Styles

In school, I was always trying to play the class clown, always been that guy that make people laugh.
— Louis Tomlinson

I wasn't really interested in things that all the kids were interested in. They were interested in football, and I was more creative.
— Zayn Malik

Wherever I went, my dad just seemed to tell people that I could sing.
-— Liam Payne

I could always hear my sister's music and I used to pretend to have a guitar and, like, perform in my mirror in my bedroom.
— Harry Styles

I'm a massive boyband fan myself, Backstreet Boys, *NSYNC....
— Niall Horan

We couldn't follow the boyband stereotypes, choreographed dance routine, then everything's the same.
— Louis Tomlinson

We're definitely going to stay together. This isn't the last for One Direction.
— Zayn Malik

Someone told me the smile on my face gets bigger
when I play the guitar.
— Niall Horan

I think there's so much feeling among young girls where
they feel like they have to be this perfect thing - and
they don't. Perfect people don't exist. Sometimes
people need to be told it.
— Niall Horan

I'm the most carefree, happy person you'll meet.
— Niall Horan

I had a girlfriend when I was about 13 but we didn't
stay together for very long and I've not really been out
with many people since. I've still never had a serious
girlfriend but I would happily go out with someone if the
right girl came along.
— Niall Horan

I've got an IQ of 40 million.
— Niall Horan

I'm not really a flirt; I just try to be myself.
— Niall Horan

I'd rather be a kid and play with paper planes, than be
a man and play with a woman's heart.
— Niall Horan

Fans always tell me I'm beautiful, but no one will ever be as beautiful as them.
— Niall Horan

I just like sitting at home, chilling and watching a movie.
— Niall Horan

Katy Perry is the sexiest woman I've ever kissed. It was amazing and very purple - she had purple lipstick on. I don't think there will ever be anything cooler than kissing her... until I marry her maybe!
— Niall Horan

I'm an emotional guy, so I don't have to worry about a girl trying to get me to open up.
— Niall Horan

I actually haven't been on many dates, but I like just chilling around at home and watching a movie with a girl.
— Niall Horan

Can clearly say Vegemite is horrible! Like tryin' new stuff though.
— Niall Horan

I get really nervous if pigeons are flying around before shows. I can't stand them after one once flew in through my bathroom window and went for me while I

was having a wee. That was enough. I think pigeons target me.
— Niall Horan

I don't want to live up to how people expect me to be.
— Niall Horan

A personal highlight was probably when we got a No. 1 in the U.K. and when the album went to No. 1 in America. The top four that week was us, Adele, Guns N' Roses and Bruce Springsteen. It was ridiculous seeing those names there. Being the first band from the U.K. and Ireland to go to America and debut at No. 1 is just unbelievable.
— Niall Horan

You have to think outside the box! Can you imagine One Direction and Eminem?! That would be hilarious.
— Niall Horan

Queuing tips for fans: wrap up and bring food!
— Niall Horan

Can clearly say Vegemite is horrible! Like tryin' new stuff though.
— Niall Horan

The bigger the crowd the better really! The noise calms your nerves.
— Niall Horan

I'm quite claustrophobic, and I don't like everyone crowding around and shouting the same questions.
— Niall Horan

I don't see how you could get used to people screaming in your face, and anyone who says different is lying.
— Niall Horan

A squirrel attacked me. I got attacked by a squirrel in Battersea Park. They're dangerous. It's rare. I've torn most of the ligaments in my knee. So no football for me. It's early retirement now. I've got a floating knee-cap!
— Niall Horan

Katy Perry still gets me every time. She's very funny in person! We met at the Teen Choice Awards and she pulled my cheeks apart and told me how cute I was. My life was literally flashing before my eyes!
— Niall Horan

I feel I am a little bit older. Reckon I will start growing a beard next week.
— Niall Horan

I've got my old favorites like The Eagles and Bon Jovi.
— Niall Horan

Life is funny. Things change, people change, but you will always be you, so stay true to yourself and never sacrifice who you are for anyone.
— Zayn Malik

Just because you don't have a prince does not mean
you are not a princess
— Zayn Malik

No matter how hard life is, don't lose hope
— Zayn Malik

My biggest turn off is being a basic bitch. Damn, I hate
basic bitches.
— Zayn Malik

Life, is hard, but if it weren't, where would the
challenge be?
— Zayn Malik

my mum doesn't have a twitter account, she dont even
know how to use a computer hahahaha :) x
— Zayn Malik

Funny how everyone hates Muslims because of a few
attacks. We need to open our eyes to who the real
terrorists are.
— Zayn Malik

I'm talking about Harry so much these days, but my
love to — Liam Payne will never change aha ;)
— Zayn Malik

Stop worrying about someone that isn't worried about
you. Never leave your key of happiness in someone
else's pockets x
— Zayn Malik

Live for who you are and what you love.
— Zayn Malik

— Harry Styles Hahaha i don't really consider myself as a celebrity, i still wear my old dirty converses! you forgot to mention your old dirty socks too! ;)
— Zayn Malik

Once I was taking shower and heard a noise, so I opened the curtains and there was Niall sitting on the toilet. He just said Hi.
— Zayn Malik

Home Sweet home, i've missed London! and someone special to me :) x
— Zayn Malik

I was gonna say 'great', but then I said 'good', so I say 'groot'
— Zayn Malik

Once you learn to truly appreciate what you do have then you can begin to deserve what you want. x
— Zayn Malik

Wrote my first song ever today alone, maybe i'll sing it someday when i go solo hahaha who knows :) x
— Zayn Malik

There comes a day when you realize turning the page is the best feeling in the world.
— Zayn Malik

I didn't really enjoy her fainting in front of me, it wasn't something that I enjoyed. However, it was pretty cool to know that I could make a girl faint. I'm not gonna lie.
— Zayn Malik

No matter how hard life gets never give up
— Zayn Malik

Niall once argued with an airport security guard for 30 min so he could bring food on the plane.
— Zayn Malik

Now that I have my Rose, I really do have everything I could ever want, I have family, romance, friends, fans, and im just surrounded by love.
— Zayn Malik

Louis ate Niall's last chips when Niall went to the toilet, and Niall didn't talk to Louis for an hour...
— Zayn Malik

My favourite one in the group was Zayn, until he stole my meal. Now Harry is my favourite.
— Niall Horan

Once I tried to eat without a spoon for a day and it was really hard. Liam is the man!
— Zayn Malik

It doesn't matter what other people think about you. The only thing that matters is that you are happy with who you are.
— Zayn Malik

The sun is shining, it's a beautiful day, nothing like spending the day with your friends, and talking all night to someone you love.
— Zayn Malik

If Niall gives you his last chip you must be really special.
— Zayn Malik

If I find the girl of my dreams, I would do anything for her.
— Zayn Malik

When Justin Bieber was following me, Niall sang That Should Be Me and when Justin Bieber followed him, Niall sang Never Say Never.
— Zayn Malik

Zayn has the most swag.
— Liam Payne

The person who will give you unexplained happiness will also give you unexplained sadness.
— Zayn Malik

Never live life in fear of death.
— Zayn Malik

Before you judge people, judge yourself.
— Zayn Malik

I've smoked since I was about 15.
— Zayn Malik

I had a dream that we had a new sixth member, for some reason, and it ended up being quite horrible. And he started a fight with me, and I wanted him to go away, and none of the boys were helping me.
Luis

(Zayn) He's my best mate. I've got to look out for him.
— Liam Payne

I always wanted a brother, and now I get to chill with these guys all the time.
— Zayn Malik

You should never settle for what you get, but fight for the best you could ever have. :) x
— Zayn Malik

Liam, Harry, Niall and Louis, 'my Brothers from another Mother' - 'vos apnin boys?!' I intend to remain friends with you for the rest of my life...
— Zayn Malik

Every kiss feels like the first, Every smile is filled with the same happiness, Every laugh pulls us closer, Every time I say I love you I mean it even more :) x
— Zayn Malik

My fans kind of wear like varsity jackets and stuff. And yeah, it's really cool.
— Zayn Malik

My Grandma's operation was successful, thank you Allah :) x
— Zayn Malik

Big Bang Theory is hilarious aha!
— Zayn Malik

Don't call a girl a flirt when she's just being nice, and don't call a girl obsessed when she's just in love.
— Zayn Malik

I don't need the perfect one. I just need somebody who will make me feel like I'm the only one.
— Zayn Malik

Life is to short to be anything but happy. So take what you have and make the best of it.
— Zayn Malik

The challenges aren't there to stop you...they're there to help you grow
— Zayn Malik

She ripped out my heart, and threw it away. Given up on love, I just wanted to say. I love you, its true, there was noone but you.
— Zayn Malik

It's cool to know that I can make girls faint
— Zayn Malik

Dreams always come true, if you only believe.
— Zayn Malik

Faith can really help get you through the hard times.
— Zayn Malik

Liam is our daddy, he takes care of us.
— Zayn Malik

Unbelief will destroy the best of us. Faith will save the worst of us.
— Zayn Malik

Life is a gift, love it, live it.
— Zayn Malik

It hurts seeing a girl cry. I want to comfort them for as long as I can, or I'll end up crying too.
— Zayn Malik

Don't depend on someone promising you the world. Fulfill your own wishes, make your own dreams come true
— Zayn Malik

I don't eat pig, so I've got chicken. Special chicken.'cause I'm special.
— Zayn Malik

The hardest challenge is to be yourself in a world where everyone is trying to make you be somebody else
— Zayn Malik

Don't live in the past. You might miss the great things happening in your present.
— Zayn Malik

Good decisions come from experience, and experience comes from bad decisions.
— Zayn Malik

Liam, Harry, Niall and Louis are my brothers from another mother.
— Zayn Malik

You make life out of what you have, not what you're missing.
— Zayn Malik

Learn to appreciate what you have before time forces you to appreciate what you had
— Zayn Malik

Louis knows, I'm Bruce Lee
— Zayn Malik

Louis, back me on this one. When we have a playfight with Zayn he never loses, he never gets hurt, does he? He's always like the most powerful person.
Liam

I really shouldn't be saying this, but once me and Liam were fooling around and we ended up kissing
— Zayn Malik

Zayn encourages me to go out with girls, but i say my princess is on her way. I have to wait.
— Niall Horan

If I find a fan attractive, I'll let them know
— Zayn Malik

Life is funny. Things change, people change, but you will always be you, so stay true to yourself and never sacrifice who you are for anyone.
— Zayn Malik

There comes a day when you realise turning the page is the best feeling in the world, because you realise there's so much more to the book than the page you were stuck on.
— Zayn Malik

'You and I, we're about to make some memories tonight' :) x
— Zayn Malik

Just close your eyes and enjoy the roller coaster that is life :) x
— Zayn Malik

I gave Niall a key to my house for emergencies. I found him eating my food and he said It was an emergency, I almost starved!
— Zayn Malik

We don't mind having haters. As long as we have our girls, we are strong
— Zayn Malik

The luckiest girl in the world would be Niall's future girlfriend
— Zayn Malik

No matter how hard life is, don't lose hope
— Zayn Malik

My faith means everything to me, god is sending me on this journey, this discovery, of who I am, and I trust his judgement. x
— Zayn Malik